CONTENTS

FREE GIFT	v
A Note About Links	vii
Introduction	ix
1. The Conveyor Belt Process	1
2. Plan Your Book	6
3. Speak Your Book	15
4. Editing	21
5. Final Book Content	30
6. Front Matter	32
7. Back Matter	38
8. Format Your Book	44
9. Releasing Your Baby into The World	48
One Last Chance	57
Found a Typo?	61
About the Author	63
Books by Jonathan Green	67
One Last Thing	71

FREE GIFT

Are you ready to turn readers into raving fans who are absolutely dedicated to you as an author? Would you like to get amazing reviews and support for your future products?

Then you need to TRAP them!

https://servenomaster.com/trapped

The TRAP System is a two part system to help authors like you turn readers into raving fans.

1. Kindle Compatible Opt In Template

This is a special page that works INSIDE of a Kindle. To see how it works, just click the link on this page.

Your readers don't need to put down your book and go to their computer to give you their email address - they can do it when they are most excited by your amazing content.

The easier it is for a reader to take action, the more likely they are to do it.

2. 7-Day Email Sequence

This perfectly crafted sequence includes a Fiction and a Non-Fiction version.

These emails engage with your readers and get them to follow you on social media and leave a powerful review for your book.

These emails are perfectly designed to maximize your success as an author.

https://servenomaster.com/trap

A NOTE ABOUT LINKS

Throughout this book, I mention other books, images, links, and additional content. All of that can be found at:

ServeNoMaster.com/Authorship

You don't have to worry about trying to remember any other links or the names of anything mentioned in this book. Just enjoy the journey and focus on taking control of your destiny.

INTRODUCTION

When I was in high school, a teacher once asked me how many kindergartners I thought I could take in a fight.

I was 16 years old and full of vinegar. With two years of Tae Kwon Do lessons under my belt, I was pretty sure I could win a fight with a kindergartner.

But then he said, "Let's imagine you're on the stage in the auditorium, and ten kindergartners come at you. Do you think you could handle that many if they piled on?"

When you watch movies, bad guys always take turns attacking. They believe in a fair fight, and each henchman waits his turn to attack the hero. As a movie aficionado, this was how I first envisioned my great kindergartner battle. I would defeat one of these little rascals before taking on the next one. But I was dead wrong. Kindergartners don't fight like that. Their parents don't let them watch R-rated movies, so they don't know the rules. They will rush you all at once.

While you might have a chance against ten little monsters, once that number hits fifty or one hundred, your odds of success move closer to absolute zero.

There is a value that comes from quantity, and that's

what this book is going to teach you. I want to teach you how you can release a good book every single week. It's essential that you dial into that critical element. Anybody can put out bad books all the time, but that's not what I want.

In this guide, we're going to look at limitations and possibilities and see that many of those limitations no longer exist. The assumption that writing is a slow process and books take six months or years to write is outdated. We're going to stop living in the past and start taking advantage of technology and our better understanding of human physiology and psychology. We're going to achieve some amazing and powerful things.

My books always tend to be too long because I can't stop myself. A year after publishing the first edition, I finally released the abridged version of *20K a Day*. People were complaining that the book was far too long, and they were right. That's the last book I wrote before hiring my editor.

Even though writing that book from my dock was one of my greatest experiences and marked my transition to dictation, it was still way too long.

> I want that to become your problem – that you generate too much content, not too little.

If you decide to read that book, make sure you pick the second edition: the shorter, leaner, edited-by-Alice edition. Believe me; you'll appreciate the new version.

In this book, I want to show you that you can dictate a book from scratch in just two hours because that's exactly what I'm going to do right now. This book is based on a podcast episode where I first taught this initial concept. I want to demonstrate yet again that I can do what I'm talking about while I'm doing what I'm talking about.

I want to take a moment and share with you where I am right now.

I just finished a book for a ghostwriting client. Five minutes ago, I uploaded the last file for my editor to process before we send it to the client.

I'm up in my office. It's twelve square meters on the third floor of a hostel that my wife and I bought this summer. It's open-air, and all I can see in front of me is rooftops and palm trees. It's a little bit rainy, but the view is majestic up here.

I only like to spend a couple of hours a day up here, so we often rent the space to guests at night. Up here is my slice of paradise, as I stand to face the world. In my giant view towards the ocean, I feel like I'm the captain of an airship.

I haven't done it yet, but I'm thinking about buying a boat wheel, so I can feel like a pirate driving my airship as I look at the world. That might be one step too much. I haven't decided yet, but that's how I feel up here. So far in my research, I have only been able to find miniature wheels, but I need something full sized for the desired effect. If I do manage to get one put up in here, I'll make sure to take a picture and share it on my social media channels.

This little office is as close to the heavens as I can get. I can look down on everything that's happening. I can see my kids playing, the dog running around, and guests coming and going.

As I finished my client project, I thought to myself, "I have the notes ready for this book. I feel like writing a new book. Why don't I crank one out before I go downstairs and have lunch?"

That's the power I want to give you. I want you to be able

to generate a book every time you're in the mood. There is no longer a momentous struggle, but instead, something that's so easy to do on a whim.

The average human speaks 125 to 150 words per minute. Very few people can type that fast, and usually, they are transcribing or taking notes – not creating. It's very rare to find people who can think, create, and type that fast at the same time.

The faster you can put words on a page, the faster the project is done. Speaking 150 words per minute continuously for two hours generates 18,000 words, which is 1,000 words longer than my last book.

My books now are trending towards shorter. *Serve No Master* got away with being 107,000 words, but shorter books lead to more success. Non-fiction books are trending around 20,000 to 25,000 words.

If you are thinking about writing fiction, then you need to look at writing a book in six hours rather than two because the sweet spot for fiction is about 60,000 to 65,000 words. But that's okay; that's still waking up, having an idea and being done before you go to bed.

Let's do a little math. Selling a 20,000-word book for $2.99 is far more profitable than selling a 100,000-word book for $7.99.

At $2.99, I can generate five books from the same 100,000 words. Five times three is $15. Therefore, it's twice as much profit for me to write shorter books and charge less money. I get paid more per word when books are shorter, and many people prefer shorter books.

One of the most common complaints I get is that my books are too long, and that's why I'm trending down. I hope you appreciate that this book is lean. I want to teach you this skill as quickly as possible.

Some of my books are as short as 15,000 words, and that means people can finish reading them in less than two hours. I can create something in the same amount of time it takes a single reader to consume it.

Right now, 20,000-word books are my sweet spot because they go into some special categories for short reads. Some people look to buy books based on the shortness, and I want to reach those people.

Having spent a long time writing in different modalities, I know that I can dictate four times faster than I can write by hand. While I love writing by hand, those days are behind me. A major medical issue with my eyes forced me to transition from writing on my computer to writing by dictation.

Here's the bright side though: instead of spending eight hours writing a book, I can spend two and then spend the remaining six hours with my kids.

That's my superpower, and that's what you're going to be able to do as well by the end of this book.

Writing faster allows me to spend more time with my family, away from the computer. I want the same thing for you.

Increasing your efficiency will allow you to earn the same amount of money in less time. That's the ultimate dream. We want to make more money and have more time to do the things we love.

Imagine if you could accomplish everything you do in an eight-hour day in just two hours. That's how much you can increase your efficiency when you transition to the two-hour book method. You can choose to work four hours a day, which means you get four hours of free time and double your income.

Before we dig into this task, I want you to think about what you want to achieve. Knowing your goal will help to motivate you through this process. Do you want more freedom? More revenue? Do you want to accomplish four times as much and still work eight hours a day?

I greatly value the balance between the time I spend working and the time I spend with my kids. They just came and spent twenty minutes going crazy in my office in between the introduction and this chapter, and I loved it. I'm now rejuvenated and ready to dictate more.

My goal is to release a massive number of books. My old goal was fifty books, and now I want hundreds. I want as many people as possible to hear my voice, read my words, and be influenced by my philosophies.

I don't want to wait years to hit my goals; I want to be there fast. I don't want to write fifty books over my lifetime; I want to write fifty books a year. Why wait until my twilight years to hit my goals when I can hit them right now?

When you have a clear goal in front of you, you know why you're writing.

Every time you write an article, blog post or book, you should have a clear definition of why you're doing it.

What's the goal?

Far too many writers are putting out books without knowing why. Either they felt like writing something, or they wanted to tell a specific story. But we need a bigger goal than that.

I want you to write books that people want to read – books that generate revenue for you and give you more freedom and success. That's my goal for you. While your goal for yourself might be slightly different, lock into that goal, and that will help you to move towards your destination.

The ability to write faster has allowed me to release books on an exponential scale compared to last year. And that skill is only accelerating. While you can see all the books I published under my name, what you can't see are the many books I published under pen names and ghost-written for clients.

People often look at my business and say, "Wow, Jonathan, you are working on so many projects. You create so many courses, products, articles, podcasts, and blog posts. How do you create so much content?" It's simple – I'm passionate about what I do, and I'm very fast. Very soon you will be too.

1

THE CONVEYOR BELT PROCESS

Now that we've done enough warm up, let's get to the meat of the process. I structure every single book I create using my conveyor belt process. I want you to think of writing a book as a little factory, with the conveyor belt running around as your book goes through the different phases.

1. At the beginning of the conveyor belt is where you come up with your idea. You do research and outline your book.
2. The second station is where we create the content by dictating and transcribing.
3. Then the book is edited, and the final draft is generated.
4. Station four is where the book is prepared and formatted for eBook distribution.
5. At station five we create the paperback version.
6. Then we convert our book into an audiobook, find someone to be the reader, send them the script, and hire them.

7. And finally, we create the hardcover edition.

Of course, you can add more stations as you grow. Whether you're creating motivational cards based on your book, a journal, or even a board game, all of those things are possible once you have a strong process. But let's start with our initial seven-step conveyor belt.

Most people look at this description of these seven phases and say, "Wow, that must take forever!" If you did them in order, one step at a time, it would take an eternity. However, we can hire a person to work at each station, so that we achieve processes simultaneously rather than one after the other. Our goal is to create a process where we always have multiple books in development.

Henry Ford invented the conveyor belt to build cars. Conveyor belts, robots, and building machines are so ubiquitous now that we often forget how things used to work. Before he invented the conveyor belt, one person would build the entire car from scratch. As soon as they finished one car, they would start making another from scratch, and so on.

This process was extremely slow because one person had to be a specialist at everything from installing tires to connecting radio wires.

Instead of being specialists at everything, we want to develop a process where a new book is coming off the presses every few days. We can bring in software tools, outside help, and experts to fill in each different station of our conveyor belt

One of my friends runs a publishing house. He doesn't write books, so he outsources that part of the process. There's one person who comes up with the ideas. Once those come in, he sends them to his team of writers and assigns a different book to each writer. They're all working on a staggering scale so that a new book gets completed every week. He also has other experts on his team who record audio books, transcribe, and edit.

I want you to see that this can either grow into a full-fledged, powerful business or stay small and tight as I prefer it; quickly and efficiently generating all of your content only.

I'm continually planning future books. I keep notebooks with me, and every time I have an idea for a book, topic, or title, I write it down. There are certain times where it's impossible for me to dictate or pull out the laptop, so I work in my notebooks.

Once I have a massive list of book titles, I write the outlines. As I write the outlines, I have a vision for which books I'm going to work on next, and I know if I need any research. I can go to the dictation process once the outline is done.

I dictated this book today because I was in the mood, not because I needed to. I selected this from over fifty completed book outlines.

Right now, I have enough outlines to write a book a week for the next two years, without having to come up with a new idea. As part of the concurrent process, once I come up with the titles for my books, I start sending ideas to my cover designer. This is book one in a twenty-book series. After a day where I had great inspiration, I have outlined most of the books in that series and have all the book covers completed.

As you're writing and growing your business, you will discover that people sometimes respond to different ideas, and that's when you pivot. Because I have fifty books outlined, when I find out that some will not hit right away, I can easily switch and work on something else. I have enough things prepared that I'm continually cycling.

My goal is to always have these things ready: titles to outline, outlines to dictate, recordings for my transcription and editing team, edited books for a final review, and final books undergoing formatting for launch.

I'm also working on a fiction series. That's my passion project. While I haven't fully outlined beyond book one, I have the rough outline and titles done for the next nine in that series. I've already started the cover creation process for that series as well.

The reason we use concurrent processes is so we never hit a bottleneck. There's nothing worse than finishing your book, being ready to release it, and then realizing you haven't started the cover creation process. If it takes you a month to create a cover, you will have lost a month of opportunity, sales, and productivity. I never want that to happen to you.

You can start as a one-person operation where you're doing everything yourself. You want to continually cycle throughout the day so that you're allowed to be driven by your moods and inspiration. If you're in a dictation mood, you should be able to do that rather than being held up by another book that's frozen the process.

When you want to dictate but have no outlines ready, want to outline but have no book ideas ready, want to edit but have no books ready for editing, that becomes your bottleneck. You end up doing what you have to do rather than doing what you want to do. This decreases your efficiency and happiness, and that's the opposite of the conveyor belt method.

As you develop your process and refine your conveyor belt, you'll become more efficient and find the method that works for you. I've gone through many different processes and team configurations over my writing career because I'm constantly changing how I write, how I interact with my team, and what creates the greatest efficiency for us.

I want you to see that not only is the conveyor belt system fast, but it's also modular. You can use it in the way that suits you best based on how you create.

2
PLAN YOUR BOOK

My process begins with the idea phase. I like to write down book titles first for my ideas – even though, by the time the book is finally released, the title is often completely different.

My first big success online was a book for women about how to get their boyfriends to propose. It was called *The Boyfriend Project* in all of the initial documents. Obviously, that didn't become the final title. Instead, the final release version is *Girl Gets Ring*. I like to write down titles because it gives me a feel of what the book cover's going to look like and what I'm going to be creating. As that book grew beyond a boyfriend management system and into a way to go from dating to engaged, the title grew as well.

I get ideas from many different places, and I have written many kinds of books. Lately, I have had a lot of success publishing coloring books. They are a blast and doing really well for me right now.

One day, I sat down and wrote down about fifty different creative coloring book ideas I had, so the conveyor belt would never get stuck at the idea station. That's a page of my notebook. Every time I start working on a coloring project, I can select one.

This project started with the idea that I would like to have a twenty-book series on authorship. I teach a lot about the power of the series; it's the best way to achieve massive success with your books. And yet, I don't have a lot of series.

While it's more important in fiction than non-fiction, the principle remains the same. That afternoon I came up with an idea and wrote down twenty titles. These are the ingredients I will use as I start my next conveyor belt.

Set aside a little time every day to brainstorm new ideas and add them to your notebook. Sometimes it takes months for an idea to move into production, but having a single place where all your ideas are collected is invaluable. Far too many authors have just one idea and want to ride it through the entire conveyor belt process until they need to come up with the next idea.

There's nothing harder than trying to come up with a brilliant book idea under pressure. The best ideas come at the most unexpected moments. By adding in a little creative thinking time each week, you leave room for inspiration to appear in your daily life.

After the idea station, I have the table of contents station. This is where I will turn an idea into a dictatable outline.

At this station, I begin by cracking open my notebook and looking at all of my book ideas and titles. I search for a title that's either popular and trending, something one of my audience has expressed an interest in, or something I'm passionate about. I love writing and talking about writing, so creating a series about writing was a natural decision for me.

If you are already an expert on the topic, you can come

up with your table of contents straight from your head. For some of my books, I do that. If it's a topic I've written about dozens of times before, I have a pretty strong feeling. Having written over two hundred books, I have a real sense for the structure of a table of contents and how I want to organize and structure my books.

However, if I'm entering a new genre, writing a book in a new style, or writing about a topic I'm not yet an expert at, I'll start with competitor research. That means looking at the table of contents of your competitors or other books that are popular.

Look for books whose readers you want to read your books. You're going to do is merge the best five or ten tables of contents into your table of contents. This will be the skeleton of your book. It will give you an idea of what people expect, in the same way that nearly every movie follows the same three-act structure. It's the same series of events. We all know that in a romantic comedy, about seventy percent of the way through the movie, the main characters will break up and their relationship will enter a state of turmoil. This is so that the book or movie can end on a high note when they get back together.

Movies and books need an expected structure. Writers have already figured out what people respond to, so you don't need to create your idea from whole cloth. Instead, you're going to take the bones, the structure, and the beats of a successful story and lay on top of it your knowledge, interpretation, and facts.

Nothing I teach in any of my books, courses, blog posts, or podcasts is original. I am a commodity. There are other books on dictation, and there are other people with podcasts. There are other businesses with similar content to mine. The difference is my personality, my interpretation, my metaphors, and my way of storytelling. It's what I add on top of it.

There's a reason that you can't copyright the drums in any song. You can take the drumbeat from any song you like and write your song on top of it, and you'll never get in trouble. But if you touch the baseline or the guitar, well, that's the special sauce. That's what you're going to bring to your book.

Once you have a ton of ideas for books, continually move ideas up and down that list and create tables of contents for them.

As you're researching for your book, you can look at the length of all the books written by your competition. There are certain categories where length is fundamental. As a fiction consumer, the longer the book, the more I like it. I like to read science fiction, space marine, and space navy books. The longer, the better because I read very quickly. While a 200-page book might keep someone else entertained for days, it's only going to fill in one afternoon for me.

But when I'm looking at books to write and genres to enter, I'm focusing more and more on shorter and more efficient content. If you find a book that you want to write, but it needs to be 60,000 or 100,000 words, either break it down into a trilogy or move something else to the top of your tree. That way, you can be as efficient as possible. Lengthy books take lots of time and make less money.

If you can crank out a book in a two-hour morning session, then you can move that to the next station in your conveyor belt. But if you have to spend two hours a day for an entire week, it's going to start gumming up the works.

I'm not against writing longer books. I simply want to walk you through why I'm focused on shorter books right now.

I've seen an increasing number of books, products, and training on how to avoid writer's block. That market seems to be exploding.

This chapter could have been called avoiding writer's block, but that's a negative title. I prefer to say something positive and focus on the good. When you hit writer's block, it is always caused by bad preparation. You didn't outline, you didn't research, you didn't take enough notes, so you don't know the next decision you're going to make.

When you're writing and creating a book, there are two different phases. The first phase is the decision-making phase. This is where we outline, research, put together all of our notes, and assemble what's going to happen in the book. We design our characters and create our worlds. We put in the order of chapters. We know which scenes follow each other and what will happen in each scene.

If you start writing by the seat of your pants, whether in fiction or nonfiction, you're not prepared. You'll hit a moment where you don't know what's supposed to happen next, and you switch from creative to decision-making mode. Logical though uses a different part of your brain than creative thought. When you switch from using one region to another, there is a transition period. Trying to switch back and forth from creative to logical continually is the slowest way to write a book.

This is why if you outline and research at the same time as you're writing a book, you will be extremely slow.

Because I dictate, I don't have that option. I'm on the third floor, and all I have up here with me are my notes and my microphone. I don't have my laptop up here. I don't have any tablets up here. If I want to go back and research, or if I forget a fact or a statistic, I have to go all the way back down to my office, turn on the computer, start the research, save the note, put it back on my phone, then come back up here. What a massive waste of time!

I'll give you a secret here, so you don't make that mistake. When I run into a part of my book where I need to add a note or a piece of research, or something is missing, I skip it. I usually say, "Bracket, bracket," leave a note to my editor and close it with two more brackets. When the transcription makes it to her, she recognizes that as a note required to remind me, when I'm doing my final edits and back in decision-making mode, to research and find that missing piece of information.

It's crucial to be fastidious in your research, or you will pay the price later. If you have a well-outlined book, you can crank it out in two hours. But if you have no outline, or you don't know the order, then you're not sure what you want to write about. If you don't know the facts and the statistics, the writing process is going to take you a very long time.

An additional benefit of the conveyor belt method is the ability to pivot. Despite all your preparation, you may hit a significant roadblock in a book that you are writing. If it's not just a chapter missing from your book but an entire section, then you need time to research and decide what you want to write about or how you want to change it.

Rather than go back into research mode when you want to be creative, you can simply grab one of the other outlines from your conveyor belt and start dictating. Even though it's a different book, you are still making progress and keeping that conveyor belt running. Working on multiple simultaneous projects isn't just acceptable in this method – it's encouraged.

The conveyor belt method ensures that you never get stopped by writer's block ever again.

We live in a world where it's possible to get all the help

you need at affordable prices from around the world. Look at each part of your process and find your areas of weakness and inefficiency. Perhaps you're a good writer, but you struggle to come up with ideas, or your books lack structure.

That's okay because you can pay someone else to come up with an idea and give you the structure or the beats of a story. Some people do this all day long. It's not very expensive. They can help you with the bones of your story, and then you do the rest. You could be like my friend who hires someone else to do the writing because he's not a writer. He's a publisher.

For certain books, I'll hire a researcher to do the whole research bulk. If it's a heavy research process, I know how long it will take me. I'll often hire someone else to fill in that gap because that's a better use of my time.

Whenever you have areas where you need help, you can find software tools and services to help you. I dictate all my books, but there's no way I would ever transcribe them myself.

I've been through a lot of different processes, and if you read my older books, you'd see me talk about different methods. I've gone from having one full-time transcriptionist to someone who cleans up transcriptions to having a pre-editor. I've been through different processes because I'm constantly changing what works and what doesn't. As the software I use to transcribe gets better and better, I don't need to have people filling that gap; the software does the work for me.

I have an editor who works for me full-time, and she handles most of what happens after the dictation. She does 90 percent of the heavy lifting so that I'm always moving stuff through my phase of the conveyor belt and onto hers.

When I was going through a growth cycle with *Serve No*

Master, and I wanted to create a lot of products very quickly, I had an assistant who worked for me full-time, handling research. She would go through hours of video courses, take notes, and create long, in-depth outlines for me.

These outlines would have taken me just as long as her to create because I would have had to watch the same videos. However, because I know my field very well, I can look at an outline and, in an hour or two, remove everything I don't want, improve the sections that could be better, and turn it into a great structure.

As far as my product creation conveyor belt, I send her back the revised outline, and she creates all the PowerPoint slides that I'll use to record my videos.

While you can start outperforming every part in your process, you could also transition to a phase where you no longer need to do that. Once you know what an hour of your time is worth, and you can pay someone less than that amount to do a task, then do so. That's a win. How much would you pay to get an hour of your life back?

As part of my current process, I have transcription software that turns everything I record into text and gives all the files to my editor. She then cleans it up and sends it back to me. At the same time that process is going on, I have a full-time designer that prepares book covers, social media graphics, and everything else I need designed. That's on the conveyor belt as well.

Every time I have a book idea, I can send it to my designer to start working on it at the same time as I start the process of researching and writing. Once the book is done, I can send it on through the conveyor belt to the audiobook creation process. Once they have the final version of the book, I can also start the paperback and hardback cover creation processes.

There are many things I don't handle myself as part of this process, but they're handled efficiently because I know when and where to outsource. I don't design my book covers; it's inefficient. I don't record my books because it's impossible for me to get that much silence. You can find other people to increase your efficiency and become a book factory all on your own.

3
SPEAK YOUR BOOK

Each station on our conveyor belt can have multiple stations. When planning your book, you can break table of contents and research into two different stations.

The rules for stations aren't hard and fast. Instead, this is a modular system that you can modify to match your writing style and areas of expertise. While this section teaches my fast method for dictating books, you can still write them by hand if you prefer. It will just take more than two hours.

Speaking your book can be broken down into three smaller phases:

1. Recording the audio
2. Converting the audio to text
3. Cleaning up the text

You can break down these phases into your components, and I'll share with you a few different ways to get your ideas onto paper.

I dictate my books out of necessity. I was so passionate about writing by hand that I couldn't imagine ever becoming a dictator. But once I got through the initial bumps and developed this process, I never looked back. I can't imagine writing a book by hand anymore. Dictating is faster and a lot more fun!

You no longer require any specialized equipment to start dictating. All you need is a smartphone, a microphone you can plug into your phone and clip to your shirt, and an app that costs less than $2. That's all the equipment I use to create my books, including this one.

With this dictation method, you are completely location independent. I write many of my books walking along the beach, through my garden, or up here in my airship office. Each of these locations allows me to surround myself with nature and walk while I write. I get a little exercise in while the creative juices are flowing.

Everyone dictates in their own way, so you will have to experiment a little to find your path. I like complete isolation, so I look for spots where I can't see another human. You might like walking around the park in your neighborhood. Or maybe you dictate while sitting down. Find a way to dictate that feels natural to you and stick with it, even if other people don't understand.

When I'm dictating, I imagine that I'm telling a story to a single person. This invisible audience helps me direct my story, and that's why my books have a conversational tone. You can imagine giving a lecture to a university classroom or speaking your book in a more intimate setting. The imaginary audience will help you set your familiarity level. If you want a business book, then imagine speaking to a business audience. If your book is for kids, imagine reading to a small group of kids at a local library.

When choosing your location, try to find a place where people won't distract you, shout at you, annoy you, or overwhelm you with noise, so that the audio recordings are usable. The beauty of transcription is that it doesn't need to be nearly as pristine as an audiobook. The cleaner the recording, the most successful the transcription process will be.

The second part of this process is converting that transcription into written text. Over the last two years, I've tested every single tool out there. While some of them have been nightmares, I have finally found a system that works pretty well for me.

There are a few options that you can choose from and feel free to experiment until you find the solution that matches your budget.

Your first choice is to hire a transcriptionist. You can easily hire someone online – there are many services and platforms such as rev.com – and you can expect to pay between $1 and $1.50 per minute of recorded audio. The beauty of human transcription is that what comes out is pristine. If you dictate a book over two hours, expect to pay $120-180 to convert your book. If that price is worth your time, then this is going to get you the best final results.

I don't use this process because I create too much content. The cost would outweigh the benefits if I were transcribing thousands of minutes every single month. When you put out a large volume, hiring a full-time transcriptionist is far more cost-effective. I've worked will many full-time transcriptionists over the past few years, and I learned a valuable lesson. If you're not watching, they're not doing.

While one transcriptionist's quality started dropping through the floor, the other one started billing me for things she hadn't transcribed. My editor and I quickly caught her and asked for an explanation. She suddenly quit, as though we were the villains. That's the challenge of working with people who work remotely. They're going to get sick, they're going to have problems, and any employee needs a certain level of management.

As long as you have a good quality check process in place, you can hire a person to convert your words into text.

After my experiment with transcriptionists, I realized that the necessary oversight isn't a good fit for me. I now prefer to use software to handle my transcription needs.

There are a range of paid software solutions, and the most well-known is called Dragon Dictate. I have the latest version and use it for some of my projects. When it comes to talk-to-type, it's the best tool out there. If you want to speak to your computer and watch the words appear on the screen, it's hands-down the best option.

Dictating to your computer is not as quick as the free-form dictation style I prefer, but it is far faster than writing with your hands. There is a learning curve with this type of software as you need to learn the commands for punctuation and remember to say each command at the right spot. It can feel a little unnatural to start saying "comma" all the time, but eventually, you'll get used it.

Dictating while staring at a computer screen isn't a viable option for me. With my eye condition, I need to minimize my screen time. Whether I'm writing or talking, looking at the screen is what hurts me, so Dragon Dictate is not a viable dictation option for me.

The advantage of this platform is that you only have to pay for it once, while other solutions tend to charge based on how many minutes you are transcribing.

I prefer to remain untethered from my computer. I write my books using only a smartphone and a microphone. I want to go to different islands, hang out on the beach, spend time with my kids or come up to my office and dictate. To do that, I use automatic transcription.

Rather than embed punctation into my recordings, I simply tell my books to an imaginary friend. I take the audio recordings and upload the files to online software that processes and stories and turns them into text.

Unfortunately, Dragon Dictate does not do this well. What you get is a jumbled mess with no punctuation, no paragraph breaks, and at least one out of every twenty words will be a mistake. When I'm looking at the computer screen, I have a very high-efficiency ratio with Dragon Dictate, but when I'm not the error rate skyrockets. This is why you either want to hire a person or use tools that charge by the minute.

There are a couple of tools that are quite good out there. Right now, the three tools I'm the most familiar with are Trent, Temi, and Descript. Trent is the most expensive. At their absolute lowest rate, they charge $0,16 per minute. Temi is kind enough to charge a flat 10 cent a minute; Descript is my new favorite tool.

I've been using Temi for about a year and a half now. I love it. I love everything about it. With Temi, I can upload videos and Dropbox links, so that anyone who's editing can see my face if it's a video recording or the notes that it goes with the recording. That's far more effective than just hearing the audio. Video provides additional context and anyone cleaning up a transcript has to ask me what I meant far less often.

While I have been using Temi for a long time, I've recently transitioned to Descript and been very pleased with the experience. While the first version of the software could only handle audio files, the software can now easily handle all my video content. Descript has better sharing options and the same accuracy rate as Temi. It's super-fast, super-efficient, has amazing sharing abilities, and handles video beautifully.

When you submit your raw audio files, you get paragraphs with intelligent splits and punctuation. While it's not as good as a human, at less than ten percent of the price, the quality is exceptional. The error rate with pay-per-minute software is significantly lower than with Dragon Dictate.

Descript is even cheaper than Temi, and you get 100 free minutes of transcription when you use my link: ServeNoMaster.com/descript. If you can't remember the link, don't worry. You can find it on the toolbox page of my website. We each get 100 free minutes when you give this software a spin.

Who doesn't love free transcription? That means that you can try this entire process, create your first book, dictate for 90 minutes and get it transcribed without spending any money.

This software is only going to get better over time as more and more people use the platform and edit their books inside of the Description editor. As you make corrections inside their editor, the software learns. The error rate is always decreasing, and that's why I encourage so many people to give it a try. The more people using the software, the better it becomes.

If you decide to write your book by hand, you may skip most of this section. But now it's time to come back to the conveyor belt. Whether you wrote your book by hand or used the transcription process when you have that first draft complete it's time to head over to the editing station.

4

EDITING

My philosophy and strategy for editing have changed a great deal throughout my writing career. What I want to share with you is the most cutting-edge, efficient, and effective strategy, so you don't get bogged down. This is your chance to learn from my mistakes and avoid having to learn the hard way.

If you made mistakes in the transcription phase, this is where they will bite you. A bad transcription can bog down the entire editing process and gum up the gears on your conveyor belt.

When I wrote *20K a Day*, I dictated far too much content. I then ran it through Dragon Dictate and came up with a mess. Imagine walls of text that were thousands of words long without a single paragraph break or piece of punctuation. Along with at least one out of every twenty words completely wrong. Initially, I tried to hire editors to clean up the mess, but it was unworkable.

One of Dragon's greatest weaknesses is the lack of an editor. The software doesn't sync up the audio and text in a single dashboard for easy editing like pay-per-minute tools do.

Eventually, I had to hire transcriptionists to convert the original audio recordings because the Dragon Dictate version wasn't good enough.

My mistake in the previous phase gummed up the works in my book factory. The book launch was significantly delayed, and the final book was cumbersome and far too long. Even though the content in it is awesome, version two of that book went through my new editing process.

The first and most important thing to understand is structure. Often, the biggest mistake a book makes is being out of order. I'm passionate about deep outlining and mind mapping, so when my book enters the editing phase, I always want it outlined in Scrivener. No matter what a client says to me, no matter what an editor wants, no matter what anyone else who's a part of the project says, I demand that I only see the book in Scrivener format.

And that's because Scrivener allows me to create files and nested files – and nested files within those – so that each chapter can be broken down into small sections. If I want to move things around, I can drag and drop. Trying to edit in Word takes away my ability to focus on tiny sections and reorder things.

The first part of the editing process, and the most critical one, is to make sure that the structure is right. The order must be in the right place, and the scenes happen when they need to happen. Whether you're writing fiction or nonfiction, you'll often have to move things around, and it can be hard in Word. Cutting, pasting, and dragging things up and down the page is not efficient. And sometimes you won't do it, even though you know you should, because it's too hard.

Before you move on to any other part of the editing process, make sure that the structure is right. Do not start doing a line-by-line edit and then move a chapter around. Then you'll have to start over again to make sure that a story doesn't start in chapter 7 and finish in chapter 3.

Looking at the big picture seems obvious when I say it here, but I can't tell you how many times authors forget this step and end up having to edit the same content multiple times.

I never go straight from writing to editing the same book without a break. The conveyor belt is designed to prevent you from making this mistake, but I want to put this caveat in place just in case you're only using parts of the conveyor belt process but not the whole thing.

If you write a book in Word, the second you hit the end, you could scroll to the top and go, "Okay. Now I'm editing." If you do this, your edit won't be very good.

The conveyor belt process goes back and forth between the logical and creative parts of your brain with each station. Coming up with book ideas and titles is creative. Outlining and researching is logical. Writing your book is creative. Now that we are editing, you need to switch back to your logical brain.

Additionally, writing is about the transmutation of information. You are talking. It's the opposite of listening. When you are editing a book, you want to activate the logical part of your brain and look at the book just like your future readers will. This is the receptive part of your brain – listening.

When I was in my twenties, I used to listen to motivational recordings on my way to a night out. I wanted to stock up on advice and wisdom before going out and talking to ladies. I'm quite married now, but back in my single days, I wanted to figure things out. Over time I discovered that starting conversations was harder and more awkward despite all the killer knowledge in my recordings because I was in a receptive state. Switching back and forth between listening and talking is another transition that takes time.

Take a break of at least a few days between finishing your first draft and beginning the editing process. Think of this phase as the sherbet. You need to reset your palate before the next course. This is where the conveyor belt system really shines compared to linear writing. If you're writing only one book at a time, you can end up with nothing to do in this period. With the conveyor belt system, you can work on other books at other stations while you are giving your brain time to reset.

This is a great time to brainstorm new book ideas, outline the next book in your series, or work on book cover designs. All of these actions will help prepare your brain for the editing process.

The second reason to put some space between writing and editing is memory. When you start editing too soon, you can remember everything you wrote, and this will affect how you edit. You will start to think, "Does this happen later in the book or did this happen earlier in the book?" You will mingle memories of what you wrote at the end of the book with chapters that you edited at the start of the book.

This will cause problems and slow down your editing process. You won't be as happy with that final product.

You know that I love to complete books as quickly as possible, but I learned these two critical lessons the hard way. Putting a break in between writing and editing actually increased how quickly I complete books.

The editing phase is the first place where it's tempting to start pumping money into your book. If you are a new author and writing using a linear method, you might have big dreams of dollar signs. Many new authors expect their first book to sell millions of copies and transform their lives. While hitting a homerun with your first book is pretty awesome, it's also unlikely. The baseball players with the most homeruns often have the most strikeouts as well.

When you believe that your book is going to make you tons of money, it is easy to justify opening the vault and spending tons of money on expensive editing. Hiring a professional editor can cost you thousands or even tens of thousands of dollars.

The editor's job isn't to make readers like your book; no editor can do that. Editors are not writers. It's a very different skill. If you write a bad book, an editor will not be able to fix that, and the last thing I want you to do is to invest a large amount of money in polishing something that you don't want to release anyway. Instead, I strive for efficiency.

When I first wrote *Serve No Master*, during the pre-launch phase, I made a couple of really big changes. First, I changed the cover; the old cover was terrible. Second, less than a week before the book was coming out, someone wrote me a very mean email saying the book was so poorly edited and the grammar was so bad that I should burn the manuscript.

It broke my heart. I wanted to curl up and cry; but instead, I looked for a solution. I didn't have time or money to hire an editor with four days until launch.

There are two reasons why I don't like to work with the most professional editors. Firstly, they take ages. They are often booked out two to three months in advance. You send the manuscript now, and they go, "Great. I'll have it ready by your next birthday." Most editors take ages and are prohibitively expensive.

I want you to be profitable. I don't want you to spend more money on your book than it makes back for you, and an editor shouldn't take away all the profits from your hard work. While I use a professional editor as part of my process now, that's not how I started.

For new authors, I recommend software solutions. After receiving that brutal email before the *Serve No Master* launch, I grabbed a piece of software called Grammarly. It's a very powerful tool. I have a very detailed review of both my experience and the software on my blog. Grammarly helped me by pointing out every single mistake and every part it wasn't sure of. It's a wonderful tool as long as you work with it cooperatively.

While it will not replace a professional editor, it will do 90 to 95 percent of what a professional editor will do, and it will get your book close enough to the finish line that you won't get negative reviews that say the grammar was terrible.

Grammarly will at least get you that far. I have been using Grammarly daily ever since that happened to me more than two years ago. I more often use it to edit when posting on forums and blogs because it will point out mistakes as I'm writing in real time, and I love that.

It is a great tool, but I'm currently shifting to a new tool called ProWritingAid that has some major advantages over Grammarly.

The first advantage of ProWritingAid is that you pay once and get a lifetime license. Grammarly has a yearly subscription fee, and while the software is worth it, if I can get the same features for less money, I'm into that.

Secondly, ProWritingAid has already started adding new features – it checks for more things, finds more discrepancies, and it's becoming better every day.

Both ProWritingAid and Grammarly have free versions, and I absolutely recommend that before you start editing anything, you download both of these tools.

As much as I would love to get an affiliate commission for selling you a copy of Grammarly or ProWritingAid, you probably don't need to pay. The free versions are really good. Download the free versions, install the plugins, and check out what they can do.

Obviously, I do appreciate it if you use the links on the resources page of my website, but it's even more important that you get the right tool.

Lately, my editor has switched to using ProWritingAid more, so I have a feeling that's the tool that you will prefer as well.

Each of these tools will allow you to edit faster and more efficiently. They'll save you massive amounts of time. Instead of doing a cleanup, and then a rewrite and structure edit, and then a grammar edit, you can do it all at once using either of these tools.

The power in these tools is not that they will correct all your mistakes. They will find loads of them, and that's useful. But even more powerful is the grey area. They will flag anything that seems repetitive or like it might be a mistake. Those flags always inspire me to improve those sections, and that leads to a better final draft.

There's a time and a place for working with professional editors. Alice is my professional editor. She works full-time, and she's awesome. I only brought in Alice when my conveyor belt got so busy that it made sense to bring someone in to edit for me full-time. I auditioned hundreds of people before hiring her.

If you're looking for a professional, and it might be just for certain projects, you want to look at how much they cost, how long it takes, and what their output looks like. I sent out a sample of about two pages from one of my books to hundreds of potential editors. Nearly all of them made mistakes or sent back something so heavily edited that you wouldn't know I'd written it. It looked like a computer had written it.

You want to find an editor who can clean up your book without killing your voice. That's the sweet spot. When you do find it, that editor can help to speed up your conveyor belt. It's allowed me to accelerate my business because I only have to handle the writing part. You can choose which part of your conveyor belt process is the most important to you and which parts you want to hire other people to handle.

I already had a few bestsellers under my belt before I hired a professional and by that time I knew what I could earn from a book. My numbers were based on track record rather than speculation. The best strategy is to edit your first book yourself using ProWritingAid. If the book needs a professional touch, wait until the first edition has made some money and use those profits. Then release a new, professional-edited edition – as I did with *20K a Day*.

Your editing conveyor belt may have multiple stations. Normally, I upload my raw audio files to Descript, and then Alice takes over. Whether she cleans up the transcription herself or hires a subcontractor, she is in charge of the editing phase. Once the first edit is complete, she sends me back an edited rough draft in Scrivener format.

I then go through and rewrite that draft in Scrivener. I'll make big-picture changes, clean up some phrasing and make sure that the book has the flow I want. This rewrite is not about fixing grammatical mistakes but filling in holes in the narrative. It's mostly a creative process for me, as I can end up writing thousands of new words during this phase.

Sometimes a book needs to rotate back and forth between edits and rewrites a few times. That's ok. It's all part of the process. As you gain experience, you will get better at this process. As an early writer, I often went through three edits and three rewrites. It took marathons for me to slog through those editing sessions. With experience, I've improved my internal efficiency. Now it's quite rare for a book I write to even need a second rewrite.

For most of my books, I complete a single rewrite and send it back to Alice for a final edit. Mostly she's editing all the new sections that I've written. And then the book is ready for formatting.

FINAL BOOK CONTENT

Once your book has gone through the editing process and is ready for release, you need to prepare your final manuscript. You need to create a book that's ready to show to the masses. That means it needs to have front and back matter.

The front is everything that people read before they get to your introduction. The back is everything that comes afterward.

I use a tool called Vellum to format my books, and I've used it for a very long time because I love it, but you can just as easily export your digital and paperback formats using Scrivener.

You don't have to pay for an expensive formatter, and I never recommend that because it's another place your business can end up in the money hole. If you hire someone else to format your book, they usually send you back an uneditable version. If you find a typo or want to make any change, you have to pay them the entire fee all over again every single time.

It's very important to be strategic with the beginning and the end of your book because that will determine whether or not people join your email list, remember your name by the second book in your series, or leave a review. We want all those things to happen.

6
FRONT MATTER

The beginning of the book is important. You will need several of these pages for legal reasons and others to maximize your success as an author. You may find a different order or formula that you prefer, but this is how I start all of my books.

The very first page in your book will have the title of the book and other vital information. Originally, this was because books would often lose their covers. While this isn't as common as it was before the advent of digital books, it's still how all books start.

This page should have the title and subtitle of your book, the names of all contributors and the name of your publisher. You can also include the series name and number on this page. Think of this as a backup for the cover of your book.

It's very important that your book include this page. It's where you'll put the ISBN for your physical editions, which is an identification number assigned to every single book. While two books might have the same title, they will never have the same ISBN.

The paperback and hardback editions of the same book will have different numbers as well. These identification numbers are important as they are the real way that book sales and ownership are tracked. In the same way that two people with the same name will have different Social Security numbers, two books with the same name will have different ISBNs.

Do not try to write your copyright page from scratch. Find one at the start of a book that you like and copy it. This isn't plagiarism as it's a legal statement. This is where you tell people that you own your book and that they can't use your content without your permission. You will also include the publication information, the language, and which edition this is.

This page doesn't require a lot of creativity, so just copy a good one. Feel free to copy mine if you like.

As far as the ISBN, do not fall into the trap of buying one. You don't need to spend money here.

For new writers, this is another place where people try to take advantage of you. First of all, in most other countries, ISBNs are free. Only in America are they prohibitively expensive. A single ISBN will cost hundreds of dollars, and if you buy it through another service, such as your printer, they might charge you as much as three hundred dollars. They make a massive profit because they pay $1 to $2 for a number you don't need and resell it to you for hundreds.

Recently, the main ISBN website was hacked. Everyone who bought one for eight months had their credit card numbers stolen. No one was told until long after they'd already discovered the breach. As I'm working on this chapter, their website has been down for almost two months.

I only use ISBNs for hardback editions because I print them from a third-party printer. That third-party printer offered me a single ISBN for $275. However, I bought 100 at $6 each. I purchased 100 ISBNs, fortunately before the website was hacked, for the same price that my hardback publisher would have sold me two.

You don't really need hardback editions until you grow to a certain size. I only launched a hardback edition for my biggest book *Serve No Master* last year. While it can feel really exciting to have an ISBN for your digital book, you don't need one. With most on-demand printers, you don't need one for paperback editions either.

Delay this expense as long as possible so that the distance to profits remains as short as possible.

Every book should start with an outline of where the book is beginning and going. The value of a table of contents is often forgotten.

If you're writing a nonfiction book, it helps you to look back and see which section you liked when reviewing the book down the line. For a fiction book, especially an eBook, sometimes you might need to jump around chapters.

When I move between devices, sometimes they don't sync right, but if I know which chapter I'm coming from and going to, it's easy to jump around.

You're going to create a table of contents and put it at the front of your book. You can choose whether or not to give your chapters titles and whether or not to put the page number next to each chapter.

Most formatting tools will add this page automatically – make sure you check the box that says "include table of contents in all editions."

Many books start with a dedication. This is usually the first page that your readers will look at. While it can occur after the Copyright and Table of Contents pages, most people skip over those.

When I was first writing books, I spent ages thinking of great dedications for the start of each of my books. All my early books start with dedications, but now they rarely appear in my books.

When you're putting out a book a week, it's not as meaningful as when you are putting someone's name at the front of a project that took you five years of struggle. However, this is an important section that can mean a lot, especially to your spouse, children, or anyone else who played a significant role in helping you come across the finish line.

Usually, the purpose of the dedication is to show it to that person. It will make them smile and make you feel good.

Several of my books have forewords. This is another area where new authors sometimes run into trouble. They're tempted to pay someone famous to write the foreword for their book.

When I was creating *Serve No Master*, I had the opportunity to have a minor business celebrity – someone who had been on a TV show for a while in the past – write the foreword for my book for $5,000. He even said, "Hey, write whatever you want and throw my name on it. You're all good as long as you send me the money."

I chose not to go down that route because I said to myself, "Have I ever bought a book because of the foreword?" The answer is no.

Even if my favorite author wrote the foreword to a book by someone else, it probably wouldn't get me to read it. However, I do want my book to appear in search results next to certain other authors' names, and that's why several of my books have forewords by authors who are excellent marketers; I want my books to appear next to theirs in search results. I like to approach forewords logically rather than emotionally.

For this reason, I've initiated foreword swaps. I write a foreword for an author I respect, and they write a foreword for me. If you look at the current edition of *Serve No Master*, its foreword was written a year after it was released – only after it was a big success.

You don't necessarily need to have one. But if you do it, you're going to place at the beginning of the book.

The free gift is the final and most critical part of your front matter. It can be placed before or after the foreword. Just make sure it comes after the table of contents. If you put it before the table of contents, when people read on other e-devices, they'll never see it.

Most e-devices automatically skip to the first page after the table of contents. If you're wondering why no one has ever given you their email address, perhaps no one has ever seen your free gift page.

On the free gift page, you want to give away something valuable enough that you can turn your monologue into a conversation that will encourage people to email and communicate with you. You can then tell them about your future products, your blog, your website, and the next book coming. And you can do this by offering an audio version of your book or a short story. Whatever it is, it's worth having it at the front of your book.

My first emails are all about encouraging people to finish reading the book. That's why I want to ask for their email address at the beginning so that while they're reading the book and they're most inspired, I can start communicating with them rather than after they finish reading it, and their inspiration is starting to diminish. I want to get them in the moment of greatest excitement.

There are many approaches to the free gift page and some others even put this page a few places throughout the book. There is no perfect formula, and it's worth testing different gifts and different variations to find the perfect formula for your audience.

7
BACK MATTER

The book doesn't end with that final period. This is the back matter order that I have found most successful in my writing career, and you can use it as a baseline to create your back matter.

After the conclusion of your book, the first thing people should see is a page titled "One Last Chance."

On this page, you want to say, "Hey, I don't know if you saw it at the beginning of this book, but I have a free gift available for you, and I want to remind you that it's still here. You just have to enter your email address. I'm going to send you another book for free," or, "I'm going to send you the comic book version of this book for free. I'm going to give you something of massive value as my way of saying 'thank you' for giving me your email address. I want to reward you for finishing the entire book. Here's the link."

Try to capture all the people who didn't give you their email address at the start of the book. This is the moment when people are most excited and most likely to take action. If you can turn a reader into a follower, you have a real chance of building a business. This is your final appeal: make it as compelling as possible.

After appealing for the email address, you want to let them know that the story isn't over. The most common way to do this is with a preview of the next book in your series. You can include some chapters from another one of your books.

This doesn't have to be the start of your next book. You can include chapters from the middle of the book that have maximum excitement and ideally end on a cliffhanger. While people might get annoyed when your main story ends in a cliffhanger, you can get away with it here. Think of this as including a "movie preview" at the end of your book.

When you go to the cinema, the movie starts with previews for movies and events that the movie theater, distributor and production company want to advertise. There are even local commercials before movies where I live.

But at the end of the movie, you have a chance to focus on what matters to you. Every single superhero movie now has a stinger scene at the end of the credits. This is there for two reasons – to get people to sit through the credits and to get them excited about the next movie in the series.

The stronger your preview section is, the more likely people are to buy the second book in your series.

There are two approaches to this section. You can use the soft approach and tell your readers that these are chapters from your next book, or you can be sneaky and skip the One Last Chance page and go straight into the next book in your series. I've only encountered this once in a book as a reader. I started reading book two without even realizing it, and by the time I realized I needed to buy the next book in the series to see how things were going to play out, I was hooked.

It was a little bit sneaky, but it worked. I liked the sample chapters and read the second book because of them.

Some books even include samples from multiple books by the author. You might include samples from the first book in several different series that you have written.

If this is your first book, you might not have any additional content yet. When you have some chapters from your next book, you can go back and add them to the first book. It's never too late to improve your books.

The next page I have at the end of every single one of my books is the "Found a Typo" page. When I saw this page in another author's book, I was booked. I'm not afraid to admit when someone else has a genius idea.

This page includes a very simple message:

"If you find an error of any kind in this book, please let me know by visiting [LINK]"

This link sends readers to a page on my website where they can submit any typos that they find. I love getting these emails as it allows me to improve my books continually. I want to improve as a writer and feedback is invaluable. When you find a typo and tell me, no one after you will ever have to suffer from that typo ever again. Additionally, I would much rather have someone email me than post it in a bad review with one star due to a few typos.

When you submit a typo on my website, it is converted into a priority email that I read personally. I fix the master Vellum file immediately and then push the update to all editions of the book. This ensures that future readers never have to suffer under the tyranny of that typo again.

The reader who found a typo has their voice heard, they get to make a difference, and my sales don't suffer. If you want to see it, you can go to the end of this book and click on the link on my typo page.

You should build the same page on your website so that people can help you improve your book. This is a way to get free editing from your readers as well.

There are loads of ways to write your author biography, but since most books have this page, you should as well. This is where you can include some biographical facts, stories about how you became a writer, a picture of yourself, and links to your social media profile. Find an author biography that you like and model the style.

Your readers want to feel like the book was written by a real person and this page helps them to feel this way. When they see this page, they are more likely to join your mailing list, visit your website, or read another of your books.

This section is always a challenge for me because I have to go back and change it each time I release a new book. Because I release books so frequently, the other books section is often out of date and doesn't include everything I've written.

I have a single master version of my other books page, and with Vellum, I can easily drag and drop the master page into all of my books.

While I might not push a new edition of every single one of my books immediately, since it would take me an entire day, I will have it automatically ready for the next edition. That way, the next time someone sends me a typo, and I correct that book and send it in, it already has the correct and updated other books section.

As you write more books, I encourage you to keep this page up to date.

You don't want people to think your next book is "coming soon" when it's already been released!

The final thing at the end of your book is your Review Appeal:

"Thank you for reading this book. This is the end of the journey. Please click that fifth star. Leave me a review because reviews equal more sales, and more sales equal the ability for me to write another book.

If you leave a review, I'll write the next book in the series. I can continue to support my family. If you don't, my book will disappear. No one else will see it, which means no one will buy it, which means I don't make any more money, which means I have to get another job, and I can't write any more books for you. If there are things about the book you didn't like, you can email me, and I'll fix them, but please leave me a review so I can continue to help more people.

I write these books out of passion and a desire to support my family; please support an independent author. I'm competing with published books with massive marketing campaigns. I'm a real person, and every sale goes directly to me; it doesn't go through the hands of a publisher, an agent, and ten other people working for that publishing house.

You're paying the original artist. That's why buying a book by an independent author is more valuable than buying a book by a published author. When a book goes to a big publishing house, that author only gets a small percentage of your investment. You're mostly paying for people that were not even part of the creative process."

This page is really important, and I recommend writing from the heart rather than copying a template. I follow one author who uses the technique from the ending of the *Neverending Story*. That's a great movie, and it is quite different from the book.

At the end of this author's books, he includes an additional story where characters actually talk to the reader and explain that if nobody reads the books, they will disappear into nothing. Without reviews, new readers won't find the book, and the characters will eventually die. It's intense, but it's a great way to appeal for that critical review.

Once you have completed these pages, you can use them again and again. They are important for technical reasons, but you don't have to write them from scratch continually.

With all of these pages that aren't part of your main narrative complete, you're ready to format your book!

8
FORMAT YOUR BOOK

The first time I formatted a book, it was a nightmare. While it took a bit of work, I eventually mastered the process and have never looked back. The ability to format my books keeps me agile. I can update my books and fix typos in a matter of minutes and don't have to rely on someone else.

When you prepare your book for release, you're creating a special file that has to be in the format of whichever bookstore you're using prefers. The beauty of Vellum is that it will create six different formats – one for each of the significant different bookstores – as well as a generic digital version and a PDF version you can use for a paperback and hardbacks. I bought Vellum a very long time ago, and I've been pleased with it ever since.

You can also choose to use Scrivener. You're going to take your front matter, the book content, and the back matter, and you're going to put it all in one place, either in Scrivener, Vellum, or whichever software tool you're going to use. The software is going to create your master file. Once

I've gotten to this phase, anytime someone sends me a typo, I change the Vellum file.

Fortunately, it's quite easy to export and convert a Scrivener file into Vellum, so this process doesn't take nearly as long as it used to. It just takes minutes. It's so fast that I almost don't remember it used to be a nightmare for me when I first started publishing eBooks and paperbacks.

You can outsource the formatting phase, but make sure you always get an editable format. I have people on my team who format the first version of my books in Vellum for me. I can then do the final formatting how I like and future updates, and changes are as easy as pie.

Once you have your polished files ready to upload, you have to prepare everything else you need to release your book, starting with the book cover.

I consider the book cover station to be a unique and critical part of my conveyor belt. As part of my system, I always have covers in development.

While authors who use the conveyor belt system start their cover design process long before the book is ready to publish, far too many don't. Many authors complete their manuscript and have a book ready to publish before they start the cover design process. Using that traditional book cover process can push back your book launch by two to six weeks.

When I was starting out as an author, covers would take at least a month to complete. I had to wait for a designer to become available, request revisions of the first set of designs and wait for something that got me excited. Running that process in parallel to my other writing steps keeps that time from being wasted.

I hate when I'm ready to publish a book, and I realize

the cover's not done yet. It drives me crazy because it's a bottleneck at the exit of my factory.

The cover creation process is a part of my conveyor belt. I only need to know the text I want on the cover of my book – usually, the title, subtitle and author name to start this process. I like to find a few stock photos that I find inspiring or interesting and include them when I submit my design request. Finally, I find a few book covers that have a style I want my designer to model.

Sometimes I need multiple designers and multiple mockups to get the perfect cover. This all takes time, and this is where the conveyor belt truly shines.

Once your cover is complete, you're ready for the final pieces of preparation. The last thing you need to prepare is the description you need to get your book out in the world. That means you need to know everything that's going on to the sales page: book title, subtitle, author name, series name, edition number, description, and keywords.

I spend a great deal of time researching and preparing keywords and categories so that, when I get to this phase, I already have them prepared. As part of the conveyor belt process, I often include finding keywords and categories while researching the rest of my book. The beauty of this system is that you don't have to follow a strict order.

I look for keywords, competitors and categories using a piece of software called KDP Rocket. I have tons of demo videos on my website, but it is hands down the most important tool for book research. Rather than spending hours researching manually, I can come up with perfect keywords and categories in minutes.

I prefer to prepare my keywords and categories early in the process, but I don't want to start uploading my book only to discover that I forgot another bottleneck.

The sooner you start working on your book description, the better. You can work on your description in between the writing and editing phases. The main thrust of your book will be fresh on your mind, and it's a great use of that free time.

Most booksellers will let you write your book description in HTML. That means you can use big letters, small letters, underlines and bolds to make the page look cool. When you saw the description of this book, I bet it looked pretty cool. It's not just a boring block of text. Taking the time to format your book descriptions properly sells more books, and I want you to sell more books.

Your book description must be complete before you can advance to the next section. There are some great tools out there to help you write and format your book description, including one on my website I built myself. My tool helps you write your entire book description and create the HTML at the same time. I originally made the tool for myself to put out book descriptions as quickly and as easily as possible. But now anyone can use it.

As your book description improves, so do your sales. If your description right now is boring, change it. Write a more compelling one. Your book description is not a catalog page. You're not describing the book; you want to make people want to read it, get them excited, get them motivated and pulled in.

Tell potential readers how this book is going to change their life, excite and entertain them. Think of it as a movie preview, because that's what it is. If you get someone excited enough, they'll give you a shot.

Once you have everything from this conveyor belt station done, you're ready to publish your book.

9

RELEASING YOUR BABY INTO THE WORLD

Once you've gotten this far, it's time to show your book to the world and start making sales. This process doesn't have to be scary or hard. I am going to give you a simplified version of it because this book isn't just about writing a book in two hours; I also want you to release it fast and get it out there.

The first place you're going to upload your book to is Amazon Kindle. They are the biggest dog in the room. They have the largest part of the market and control about 80 percent of the book market.

As you're going through this process, there's one crucial decision you'll have to make, and that's whether or not you're going to be exclusive. If you're exclusive with Amazon, you'll be part of the Kindle Unlimited program. That means people can read your book for free, and you still get paid, but it also means you can't release the digital version anywhere else.

If you take this path, then you're only going to go and upload your eBook in one place – KDP. You go to the Kindle KDP dashboard, upload your book once and create the digital version. Then you click another button, and they'll pre-populate the paperback edition.

The next place you visit after you've created your eBook and paperback is acx.com. This is Amazon's audiobook platform. Once your book is live as a Kindle edition, you can claim it and start the audiobook publishing process. If you're recording yourself, you will be uploading files. If you're going to hire someone else, you can then start asking for auditions, which is what I do.

It takes two to three months to get an audiobook onto the market. I usually leave a book up for an audition for one to two weeks; then the reader takes anywhere from two to four weeks depending on how long the book is. If your book is 20,000 words, they should be able to do it in two weeks.

The audiobook review process can take as little as two weeks or as long as six weeks. That's where the big buffer comes in. This is another process you start as soon as your book is live. The audiobook creation process doesn't require much of your personal time; you just have to activate it early. It's just another station on the conveyor belt.

If you're not exclusive with Amazon, then here's the rest of your process. You want to go directly to Kobo and manually upload your book through their platform. Kobo is one of the largest bookstores around the world. They have a large market share and cool promotions.

The next place you're going to upload your book to is iBooks. The first time you upload a book to iBooks, it will feel like a nightmare. I just uploaded a book last night and was reminded of how difficult they make their platform. But it's the second-largest bookstore in the world, and people will also pay more than they will for a book on Amazon. You can sell the same book for two or three times more money.

The fourth place where you should personally upload

your book is the Google Play store. It can take a while to get approved for an account, so I suggest signing up for these platforms as soon as possible. You'll notice that each of these stores has similar boxes that you have to fill in and that's why we prepared them in the previous section.

Each store takes about twenty minutes to complete a single book submission.

Once you have manually uploaded your book to Kobo, iBooks and Google Play, the next place to go is Draft2Digital. They are my preferred distributor for multiple bookstores. While they will upload your book to Google Play for you, they will also take around ten percent of each sale for doing you the favor. It's not worth the loss in profits, so do the big stores yourself.

Draft2Digital will even format your book for you, but we don't need that service because your conveyor belt already took care of it.

This is the most efficient way to get your book onto the most platforms. Now that your book is out in the world, it's time to start marketing and selling it. (I'll cover everything I know about marketing books later on in this series.)

If you write your books like you're making a handmade car, you're going to waste a lot of time. There will be inefficiencies. Those three days you need to spend between finishing writing and starting editing will be wasted because you can't do anything. I don't want that for you. That's why I believe in working on multiple projects at different phases of development. The conveyor belt system will allow you to become a publishing machine, and you can have days that are driven by either opportunity or personality.

To give you a snapshot of my day, I started this morning by answering a bunch of emails, communicating with a couple of authors and working on a promotion. Then I checked the progress of several new eBook covers in development. Some of those were good, so my designer's going to work on the next covers in that series.

Then I decided to finish a ghostwriting book I've been working on for a while.

After a long dictation session, my throat is too sore to be able to do any more dictation. If all of my projects were at the dictation phase simultaneously, I'd be in trouble. But I have several projects at the editing stage, so I can pull out my special e-ink tablet and start editing on that instead. I can then work on the outlines for some new books I want to publish.

Working on different phases allows you to constantly use your time efficiently by saying, "What's the best thing I could be working on right now?" It allows you to find balance because you can be efficient, and that's why we use the conveyor belt system.

Having lots of projects on the go means that my business is about process, not creativity. And I want you to understand the difference. Certain authors write a book every two years: that means all their eggs are in that basket. They're focused on the creative side, and some of those books are amazing, but the way they're created is slow and unwieldy.

We want to be business-centered authors, and that's why we want to be fast – so you can spend more time working on the other parts of your business. Always strive for maximum efficiency. Look at every part of your writing as a process and ask yourself, "How can I maximize my effectiveness now?"

There are parts of this process that are creative and parts that are logical. Focus on your strengths and find ways to use software or workers to keep the stations where you are weak operating.

I don't operate every station in my factory personally. That would slow me down far too much. By breaking up the book creation process into conveyor belt stations, we can build a book factory that is filled with specialists. It's far better to have ten specialists than ten generalists working in your book factory.

It's tempting to think that the future of my publishing empire is written in stone – that I know which books will come out in which order for the next two years – but that's not the case. While I use the metaphor of a factory and conveyor belts, that's not *literally* how my business is structured.

My business is modular. That means I could work on different parts in whatever order I want, and that is where the freedom comes from.

While I have massive lists of ideas and outlines, they're not set in stone. I'm not even sure about the order of the twenty books in this series. While I have the covers and the titles done, I wrote the order just as I thought of the ideas. That doesn't mean that order is locked in forever.

I have the freedom to say, "Hey, these are ten things I feel like writing about. What is my audience interested in?" If I see that they're not interested in a topic, or that a topic is not selling, then I write about something else.

Not every book or outline that I come up with will make it across the finish line. It's important to react to your audience, both to your actual followers and to the market as a whole.

If a bunch of your followers email you asking the same question, "Hey, what happened to Sam at the end of your book?" write a book about Sam because they want to read more about him. If everyone says, "Hey, I wonder what happened before this story," write a prequel.

Recently, I published my first perma-free book. I realized that there were certain author platforms I couldn't get access to because I didn't have a book that was "wide," which means available on every platform and free. I wanted to open up that door, so I had that *idea*.

I went from idea to publishing the book within about a month. The book is number one in its category now. Every day, fifty to a hundred new people grab that book and discover me. It gave me access to a whole new market.

After I outline, my plans often change when I see an opportunity in a market, and that's the other advantage of our speed. We can pivot very quickly. The speed of production allows you to react to the market faster if you discover a new hot topic everyone wants to read about. You could publish five books on that topic in the next month and suddenly dominate a new opening.

I regularly email my followers and message my Facebook group to find out what people want to learn about next. I ask them which of my ideas most appeals to them and find out what I should work on next.

I'll look at what's popular on the market. You could do the exact same things: look at which types of books are trending. So many BDSM romance novels suddenly appeared right after *Fifty Shades of Grey*. A lot of people jumped on that bandwagon and put out their own version of that books within weeks of its release.

Just because you're late to a party doesn't mean it's a bad idea. I want to write books that people want to read and paying attention to what the market wants helps me to stay on track.

I dictated this book in far less than two hours. Normally, I don't dictate my books in a single session, especially after finishing another book. But I got in the zone, and I wanted to pound through this. So not only does this book teach you how to write a book in two hours, but I actually did it.

I want you to implement the same process I use. Try these steps and experiment with the tools. The only piece of equipment that costs any money that I recommend in this entire book is Descript. If you use my link, you get 100 free minutes, so you can transcribe your entire first book for free.

Give this process a shot, and you'll see that you can create faster, more efficiently, and get back more of your time.

As you go through this process, you might discover that you want to improve further. I cover tons of techniques and strategies in other books in the series, and also in *20K a Day*, which has tons of strategies about how to write faster. But the way we find success is through experimentation.

In a couple of minutes, you're going to have the opportunity to leave a review for this book. If you read this book quickly and decide not to try anything, that's not fair. You don't know this book doesn't work unless you try. I encourage you to actually try transcribing, try the dictation software and see if you can be faster. See if moving to my conveyor belt system improves your efficiency and is a better process for writing.

If you try these things and they fail, then I deserve a bad review. But I discovered when reading reviews of *20K a day* that I usually get either really good or really bad reviews. All the really good reviews are people who tried, and the really bad reviews are people who didn't try my techniques. That's disingenuous.

I also want you to know that this is a cooperative process. If you email me, I'll reply to you the next morning. I spend two hours replying to all the emails that come in every morning. That's how I start my day because I want to be there for you.

If you join my Facebook group, if you email me and ask me questions, not only will you find support, but you'll also find specific answers to your specific questions. We'll walk you through exactly how to overcome whatever is holding you back if there's somewhere you're stuck.

I want to help you. So, please, take the time to write an honest review after you try these processes because I know they work. I'm excited to have you begin this journey with me.

I can't wait to see the books you write in two hours. And when you publish one, please email me and let me know. I will be one of your first readers, one of your first fans, and one of your first five-star reviewers.

ONE LAST CHANCE

You've made it to the end of the book. Thank you so much for sticking with me!

As a special reward, I'm going to sweeten the pot. I really want us to be friends and turn this into a conversation.

I am going to add an additional BONUS to the Trap System just for you.

If you are ready to turn readers into raving fans who are absolutely dedicated to you as an author and would you like to get amazing reviews and support for your future products?

Then you need to TRAP them!

https://servenomaster.com/trapped

The TRAP System is a two part system to help authors like you turn readers into raving fans.

1. Kindle Compatible Opt In Template

This is a special page that works INSIDE of a Kindle. To see how it works, just click the link on this page.

Your readers don't need to put down your book and go to their computer to give you their email address - they can do it when they are most excited by your amazing content.

The easier it is for a reader to take action, the more likely they are to do it.

2. 7-Day Email Sequence

This perfectly crafted sequence includes a Fiction and a Non-Fiction version.

These emails engage with your readers and get them to follow you on social media and leave a powerful review for your book.

These emails are perfectly designed to maximize your success as an author.

3. 7 Product Creation Myths

The best ways to grow your business as an author is in the relationship. When you sell a product through a bookstore, you only keep a small percentage of each sale. But when you sell directly from your website, you get to keep every single penny.

Learn how to make killer products and overcome the fear that's been holding you back with this special guide.

https://servenomaster.com/trap

FOUND A TYPO?

While every effort goes into ensuring that this book is flawless, it is inevitable that a mistake or two will slip through the cracks.

If you find an error of any kind in this book, please let me know by visiting:

ServeNoMaster.com/typos

I appreciate you taking the time to notify me. This ensures that future readers never have to experience that awful typo. You are making the world a better place.

ABOUT THE AUTHOR

Born in Los Angeles, raised in Nashville, educated in London - Jonathan Green has spent years wandering the globe as his own boss - but it didn't come without a price. Like most people, he struggled through years of working in a vast, unfeeling bureaucracy.

And after the backstabbing and gossip of the university system threw him out of his job, he was "totally devastated" – stranded far away from home without a paycheck coming in. Despite having to hang on to survival with his fingernails, he didn't just survive, he thrived.

In fact, today he says that getting fired with no safety net was the best thing that ever happened to him – despite the stress, it gave him an opportunity to rebuild and redesign his life.

One year after being on the edge of financial ruin, Jonathan had replaced his job, working as a six-figure SEO consultant. But with his rolodex overflowing with local businesses and their demands getting higher and higher, he knew that he had to take his hands off the wheel.

That's one of the big takeaways from his experience. Lifestyle design can't just be about a job replacing income, because often, you're replicating the stress and misery that comes with that lifestyle too!

Thanks to smart planning and personal discipline, he started from scratch again – with a focus on repeatable, passive income that created lifestyle freedom.

He was more successful than he could have possibly expected. He traveled the world, helped friends and family, and moved to an island in the South Pacific.

Now, he's devoted himself to breaking down every hurdle entrepreneurs face at every stage of their development, from developing mental strength and resilience in the depths of depression and anxiety, to developing financial and business literacy, to building a concrete plan to escape the 9-to-5, all the way down to the nitty-gritty details of teaching what you need to build a business of your own.

In a digital world packed with "experts," there are few people with the experience to tell you how things really work, why they work, and what's actually working in the online business world right now.

Jonathan doesn't just have the experience, he has it in a variety of spaces. A best-selling author, a "Ghostwriter to the Gurus" who commands sky-high rates due to his ability to deliver captivating work in a hurry, and a video producer who helps small businesses share their skills with their communities.

He's also the founder of the Serve No Master podcast, a weekly show that's focused on financial independence, networking with the world's most influential people, writing epic stuff online, and traveling the world for cheap.

All together, it makes him one of the most captivating and accomplished people in the lifestyle design world, sharing the best of what he knows with total transparency, as part of a mission to free regular people from the 9-to-5 and live on their own terms.

Learn from his successes and failures and Serve No Master.

Find out more about Jonathan at:
ServeNoMaster.com

BOOKS BY JONATHAN GREEN

Non-Fiction

Serve No Master Series

Fire Your Boss

Serve No Master

Breaking Orbit

20K a Day

Control Your Fate

Breakthrough

Authorship Series

Write a Book in Two Hours

Essential Tools for Writers

The Six-Figure Writer

Get Paid More to Write

The Successful Self Publisher

Book Marketing for Authors

Making a Living as an Author

The Business of Writing Books

Turning Your Job into a Writing Career

Co-Writing a Book

Seven Secrets to Writing a Bestseller

Blogging for Authors

The Writing Habit

Email Marketing for Authors

The Bestseller Habit

Dictation Machine

Book Cover Mastery

How to Write a Successful Book Series

Habit of Success Series

PROCRASTINATION

Influence and Persuasion

Overcome Depression

Stop Worrying and Anxiety

Love Yourself

Conquer Stress

Law of Attraction

Mindfulness (coming soon)

Meditation (coming soon)

I'm Not Shy

Coloring Depression Away with Adult Coloring Books

Don't be Quiet (coming soon)

How to Make Anyone Like You

Develop Good Habits with S.J. Scott

How to Quit Your Smoking Habit

The Weight Loss Habit

Seven Secrets

Seven Networking Secrets for Jobseekers

Biographies

The Fate of my Father

Complex Adult Coloring Books

The Dinosaur Adult Coloring Book

The Dog Adult Coloring Book

The Celtic Adult Coloring Book

The Outer Space Adult Coloring Book

The 2nd Celtic Adult Coloring Book

Irreverent Coloring Books

Dragons Are Bastards

Fiction

Gunpowder and Magic

The Outlier (As Drake Blackstone)

ONE LAST THING

Reviews are the lifeblood of any book on Amazon and especially for the independent author. If you would click five stars on your Kindle device or visit this special link at your convenience, that will ensure that I can continue to produce more books. A quick rating or review helps me to support my family, and I deeply appreciate it.

Without stars and reviews, you would never have found this book. Please take just thirty seconds of your time to support an independent author by leaving a rating.

Thank you so much!

To leave a review go to ->

https://servenomaster.com/authorship

Sincerely,
 Jonathan Green
 ServeNoMaster.com

www.ingramcontent.com/pod-product-compliance
Lightning Source LLC
Chambersburg PA
CBHW060141230426
43661CB00003B/512